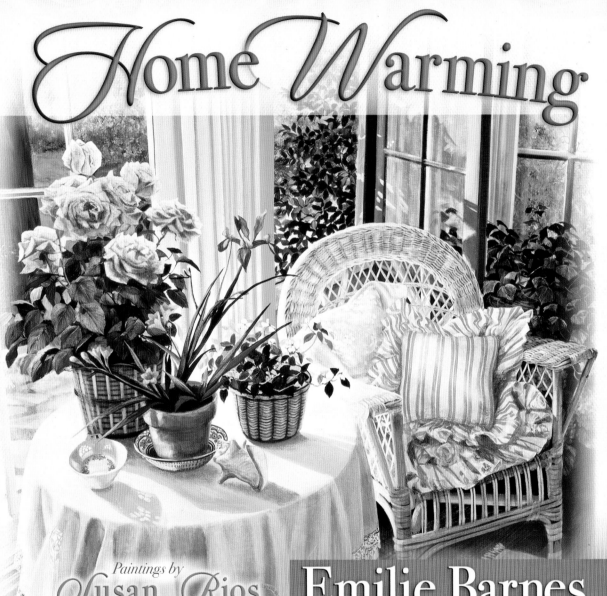

Home Warming

Paintings by
Susan Rios

Emilie Barnes
WITH ANNE CHRISTIAN BUCHANAN

HARVEST HOUSE PUBLISHERS

EUGENE, OREGON

Home Warming

Text copyright © 2005 by Harvest House Publishers
Eugene, OR 97402

Library of Congress Cataloging-in-Publication Data

Barnes, Emilie.
 Home warming / Emilie Barnes with Anne Christian Buchanan ; paintings
by Susan Rios.
   p. cm.
 ISBN 0-7369-0863-3 (hardcover)
 1. Hospitality. 2. Home--Psychological aspects. I. Buchanan, Anne
Christian. II. Title.
 BJ2021.B37 2005
 395.3--dc22
                          2004015507

Text for this book has been excerpted from *Welcome Home* by Emilie Barnes with Anne Christian Buchanan
(Harvest House Publishers, 1997).

For more information about Emilie Barnes, please send a self-addressed, stamped envelope to:

> More Hours in My Day
> 2150 Whitestone Drive
> Riverside, CA 92506

Original Artwork © Susan Rios. Licensed by Art Impressions, Canoga Park, CA. For more
information regarding artwork featured in this book, please contact Susan Rios, Inc.,
(818) 995-7467 or www.susanriosinc.com.

Design and production by Garborg Design Works, Minneapolis, Minnesota

Printed in Hong Kong

05 06 07 08 09 10 / NG / 6 5 4 3 2 1

To all my family.
Because of them, I've been motivated to make our home warm, cozy, inviting, and
happy. Thank you, sweet ones, for making me feel it's all worth it—worth the time,
effort, and hard work needed to build a nest we can all come home to.

Contents

A Home with Open Arms

Home! That was what they meant, those caressing appeals, those soft touches wafted through the air, those invisible little hands pulling and tugging, all one way!

—KENNETH GRAHAME

Don't you love that phrase "at home"?

To me it says so much about being cozy in my own nest, about being where I belong, about tending to the most important parts of my life. Being at home means savoring that sense of safety and retreat, even when I'm hard at work. The world may be whizzing by outside, but here I am safe, tranquil, peaceful, productive.

At home.

My favorite days are the ones I spend here, working side by side with my Bob or putting together a snack for our grandchildren or just puttering by myself. And I love to welcome other people in, for being at home to me is closely tied in with making others feel at home.

"Come on in," I love to tell them. "Come on in. You are very welcome here."

That's why I'm honored when a guest says to me, "I just love to come visit; it's so peaceful here." That sense of peace and rest is what Bob and I have intentionally worked at instilling.

That's why I love to say yes when friends and family ask, "May we have the party (or the meeting or the reception or, occasionally, even the wedding) here?" For many years, Bob and I have found joy in sharing our home and our life with others.

We have always wanted a home that holds out open arms to us and to others.

We have wanted a home where guests feel like family, but where family members feel like honored guests.

I invite you to come for a visit in this book, to relax and think and dream about what it means to make a welcoming home—for yourself and others. I want to invite you into my world, my home, and share with you this life I love so much. I want you to think with me about what it is that makes a house seem to open up its arms to family and guest alike.

How do you achieve a sense of welcome in your home and your life? The answers for you are as personal as your house, as unique as your personality, but I hope you will find some ideas and inspiration in this book.

Perhaps you will pick up some tips or be

encouraged to make yourself more at home in your own life. Perhaps you will simply enjoy flipping through the pages, thinking with joy and gratitude of your own "at-home" experiences. Or perhaps you will start dreaming about what you would like to do in a someday house.

At any rate, I hope that you will feel very welcome. Most of all, I hope that you will feel at home.

Make Yourself at Home

SIMPLE SECRETS OF A WELCOMING LIFE

Why do we love certain houses,
and why do they seem to love us?
It is the warmth of our individual
hearts reflected in our surroundings.

— T. H. ROBSJOHN-GIBBINGS

Some homes are places to live.

And some homes are restful retreats where you can laugh and love and work and play and dream.

Some homes offer a roof, a kitchen and bath, some bedrooms, and a couple of closets.

And some homes offer shared fellowship, peaceful silence, a comfortable chair, and a vase of flowers.

What makes the difference?

I think it's a matter of making yourself at home.

That's the *true* meaning of the word *home*making, and it's the challenge for anyone who wants to live a richer, more comfortable, and more productive home life.

From there, it's a natural next step to making other people at home as well. It's just a matter of opening your heart and adjusting your living space to make room for others.

BEGIN WITH YOUR DREAMS

You can begin or continue the process of making yourself even more at home with a little bit of thought and a lot of dreaming.

Bob and I started our life together in a tiny apartment. (It would be many years before we finally settled into the home of our dreams.) But even then we had a vision of the kind of warm, welcoming at-home life we wanted.

So we poured our energy into making that little apartment home. We had one canvas chair, a box for a lamp table, and an old trunk for a coffee table. But we had wonderful potluck dinner parties in that apartment. We invited our families over. We offered our floor (which was all we had!) for people who needed a place to spend the night.

We felt so at home and happy in that first little nest. But we were also full of dreams of the wonderful

9

subscribe to these few simple guidelines for making guests and family feel cozy, pampered, free to be themselves, free to share life together. These are the principles to keep in mind as you grow your at-home dreams into beautiful, warm, welcoming reality.

COMFORTABLE AND COZY

One vital element of "at-homeness" is simple comfort. No matter how beautiful or how fashionable your living space, it will feel forbidding if there's no comfortable place to sit.

In a living area, there should always be a comfortable spot for every member of the family, plus at least one other spot. If your budget is limited, this may have to be a goal rather than an immediate reality. But it is an important goal—one to shape your future decisions.

A physically comfortable home is carefully lit. Nobody has to squint, lean, or shade his or her eyes. And nobody has to shiver or stifle, either. A warming fire or a cooling breeze adds a lively sense of coziness, and the air is fresh, not musty. Windows open, doors close, quilts and coverlets are close at hand—and there is always a fan or an extra sweater available.

It doesn't take a redecorating job to provide any of these comforting elements in a living space, although the principle of comfort should guide any redecorating job. Physical comfort is often as much a matter of thoughtfulness and

"someday" house we wanted: a place with cool gardens and rose arbors...cozy window seats...big, comfortable sofas...rustic comfort but formal beauty.

Today, many years later, we are happily at home in a new place. The "at-homeness" we enjoy here, though, is not all that different from what we knew in that little apartment. In a sense, we have carried our home with us, because we have carried with us our dream of what welcoming living would be like.

As you dream, and as you plan and build and decorate, gradually you will find yourself more and more at home.

The result, of course, will differ from house to house, from person to person, from taste to taste. And yet I have observed that comfortable homes share certain common qualities. They

attention as it is of furniture and thermostats. Cushy sofas, glowing fireplaces, convenient lamps, and cozy cushions can all be wonderful, but the real comfort comes from noticing needs and providing for them—making people comfortable in the most literal sense of the word.

IT JUST FEELS LIKE HOME!

Something feels restful and familiar about a homey home, even if you've never been there before. There are places where you can connect with others or where you can be alone. There is a lamp at your shoulder, soft rugs to wiggle your

Express Yourself

- ☙ Break free from the mental prison of "it has to match." A variety of designs for furniture and art and accessories adds liveliness, warmth, and charm to your home.

- ☙ Handmade items—wall hangings, pillows, wood carvings, even dolls—are wonderful for creating a warm, personal look. If you don't have the time or the inclination to make it yourself, try craft sales. Select something that showcases your sense of style or fun.

- ☙ Instead of stowing away instruments, heirlooms, and collections that represent your heritage or personality, consider blending them with your décor.

- ☙ If you need an excuse to change your décor a little, try "dressing" your house for the change of seasons. For summer, take down drapes and slipcover your furniture in light, bright colors. For winter, pull out your cozy rugs and other cold-weather friends.

- ☙ Your children's art can be an untapped source of decorating treasure in your home. Frame a series of crayon drawings in matching craft-store frames and hang as a group on your kitchen or hallway wall.

- ☙ Don't let a tiny budget hold back your creativity brainstorming. Keep a notebook of ideas you like, tips from magazines, pictures, instructions, etc. When you do have the money, you'll know what you want and how to express it.

toes in, cozy afghans to snuggle up in.

You somehow feel safe, yet free to be yourself. You feel—there's no other way to put it—at home.

What gives a home these cozy qualities? Most of us respond almost unconsciously to certain elements in an environment. They are generally those things that tickle the senses and evoke an emotional response.

Beautiful colors—either cozy and warm or restful and cool—can evoke that sense of emotional comfort. Certain textures or fabric can cuddle and caress. Gentle and familiar sounds— running water, soft music, even the air conditioner—soothe the spirit and offer rest. And smells are especially evocative to most people. Though these responses are intensely personal, certain smells seem to have an almost universal homeward tug, like the smell of bread baking or the warm scent of soup bubbling on the stove.

A variety of little tricks can do a lot toward filling a home with emotional comfort. A scented candle burning on a dresser or soft pillows on the sofa are inexpensive ways of making a house feel like home. Sachets in the cupboards and the closets can replace musty smells with sweet, evocative ones, and vanilla-scented hand lotion can leave everybody's hands smelling of sugar cookies. A wool coverlet draped over the back of the sofa or a footstool nestled close to a chair—all these can add that special homelike atmosphere. Even a half-worked puzzle, a needlework project in a basket, or a book with a marker can give a house that at-home feel.

SURROUNDED BY BEAUTY

Beauty is as necessary to the spirit as food and clothing are to the body. Fortunately, beauty is easy to invite into any home, for beauty has many faces. Beauty can be found in a hand-colored photograph or a hand-stitched quilt, or in shelves lined with bright-hued jelly jars. A pot of graceful ivy can be beautiful, and so can a sweet-potato vine growing in a jar.

Even the arrangement of a home can be beautiful. When furniture and objects, whatever the cost or the style, are combined with care and attention, the result can be warmly beautiful, even if the individual pieces are less than lovely.

What is beautiful to you? What makes you smile or your spirit soar? That is the beauty that should surround you in your home, and it will be shared with all who come to visit.

Seek out beauty in whatever form it speaks to you. Surround

yourself with beauty. In the process, you will be creating something truly beautiful as well: a lovely home graced with a happy, welcoming spirit.

Personal Touches

I feel immediately at home in houses where people have surrounded themselves with what they love. I like to walk into a house and immediately have a sense of what they read, what they collect, what they like to cook, how they like to spend their time. (This gives me something to talk about as well.) I enjoy meeting well-behaved pets and seeing evidence that there are children in the home.

Our home overflows with objects that remind me of who I am and what I love. Clusters of family photos—on a wall of our great room, on a table in the bedroom, on my desk, and on the refrigerator—fill the spaces of our home with smiling, familiar faces. Teacups from my long-time collection retell their stories to me each time I look at them. My mother's secretary and my auntie's crystal build a bridge for my memories. Books and signs and plaques collected on our trips fit together like pieces that make up the puzzle of our lives.

Somehow, it all manages to come together in a homey atmosphere that says, "This is who we are. This is what we love. Please have a seat and let us get to know you, too."

Cleanliness Creates Hominess

Bob used to tease me that I would die with a broom in my hand. And it's true that the first thing I usually want to do when I come home from a trip is grab a broom and sweep off the front step. I love that sense of getting my home in order. To me, it's hard to feel comfortable and at home in a house that is dirty, cluttered, or disorganized.

Create a comfortable nest where people you love, including yourself, can work and play and relax and visit without worrying about whether they will step on a toy or be faced with a discouraging pile of undone chores.

It Takes a Lifetime

It takes a lifetime, this process of making yourself at home.

Homes grow and change just as people do. But these simple secrets of "at-homeness" hold steady through the ongoing homemaking process.

Make yourself comfortable—and create a comfortable environment for yourself and others.

Add the little touches that make a house feel like a home.

Surround yourself with beauty.

Surround yourself with *you.*

Create peace by ordering your environment.

Above all else, listen to your dreams of home. Allow them to guide you as you learn to make yourself and others happily at home.

Instantly at Home

COZY FIRST IMPRESSIONS

We welcome you most cordially.
We welcome you most regally.

—FRANK BAUM

Your mama told you that first impressions count.

But if you've always heard that as a daunting warning, embrace it now as a warm opportunity. With a little thought and a little caring, you can have a home that makes guests and family alike feel instantly at home.

Where do you begin?

In a sense, you begin at the door, or even at the curb.

More accurately, though, you begin with a hospitable heart.

You begin with a willingness to share your life, to make space in your plans for friends, family, and strangers. From there, it's just a matter of a little planning and a little creativity to make your welcome immediately obvious.

A whimsical mailbox by the driveway, for instance, can say a happy hello to anyone who approaches.

A curving walkway dotted with lamps or visited by shy lawn animals can lead the way to welcome.

A bright banner hanging in the apartment hallway can announce, "This is the right place—and we want you in it!"

Best of all, the sight of you standing at the door with a glass of warm cider or cold iced tea gives the unmistakable message: "You're welcome here. We're thrilled to see you. Please come in and make yourself at home."

A CUSTOM-TAILORED WELCOME

However it is expressed, the best kind of first impression is a personal one. It reflects your tastes, speaks clearly of your caring. When possible, it is specific to the person arriving.

The first time I visited my good friend Donna Otto's home, she picked me up at the airport and drove me through the desert landscaping to her house. The automatic garage door opener whirred, and we drove inside. And there on the wall of the garage, right next to the kitchen door, was a big blackboard with the words, "Welcome, Emmy."

What a wonderful greeting! Donna had thought ahead about how I would be entering her home, then she had arranged her greeting

to match. I learned that the little chalkboard is a family message center where notes, reminders, and "I love yous" are left throughout the day.

A welcoming touch Bob and I are fond of outside our house is the bench beside our door. It's a little like a porch swing, which I think is one of the world's great inventions—along with big, shady front porches.

A chair, a rocker, a swing—there's just something in the visual symbolism that invites people to "set a spell." But whatever greets your guests when they approach your drive or your walk or your steps, let it be personal and cheerful.

A House with a Smiling Face

A welcoming home looks well-tended and lovingly cared for. It presents a smiling, friendly face to the world.

Even if you love the studied untidiness of an

English country garden or the private loveliness of a Spanish courtyard-style home, even if you have chosen to landscape your home in native plants or have not had time to grow trees or plant flower beds, there are ways to arrange the outside for a nice welcome. A fresh coat of paint does wonders. A pot of mums or an ornamental sconce by the outside wall softens the barricade effect of a gated property.

AN OPEN-DOOR POLICY

My mama was the one who taught me the welcome of an open door. During the years after my father's death, when we lived in three rooms behind Mama's little dress shop, she always left the shop door open. In those pre-air-conditioning days, that door seemed to beckon customers in.

Many years later, when Mama lived in an efficiency apartment in a senior-citizen high-rise, she continued her open-door policy. It was known throughout the building that when Irene "cracked her door," leaving it open just a bit, anybody was welcome to come in for a cup of tea.

Your front door itself can say hello with remarkable eloquence. Even if you live in an apartment building with rows of look-alike doors, you can make your personal entrance look unique with an antique knocker. A little message board. A seasonal decoration such as a shock of Indian corn, a bouquet of sunflowers, a Christmas stocking. A classic welcome mat. Any of these beckon visitors and family inside.

Make sure your guests can easily announce themselves. Does the doorbell work? Can a knock be easily heard inside? Is it clear what visitors should do to let you know they've arrived?

THE FIRST THING YOU SEE

The first thing that meets the eye when people are entering your home (and the second thing, too) should be beautiful, homey, inviting—or all three.

The basics should be present, of course: a place to wipe feet, a place to hang coats. But beyond that, the entranceway sets the mood and sends a message about the whole house.

A neat foyer with a shiny floor, sparkling

17

mirror, and a closet for hats and coats says, "This house is orderly and peaceful."

A sunlit entrance hall graced by a hanging quilt and a winsome collection of teddy bears sends a clear message that whimsy and play are a part of your life.

A cozy apartment living room with plump cushions, soft music, and lots of candles says, "Come right on in and let us get to know you."

And, of course, the smell of something wonderful on the stove sends an unmistakable welcome message to anyone who steps over the threshold. I know of more than one person who has managed to sell her home quickly by popping a loaf of bread dough into the oven before prospective buyers showed up.

A Welcoming Message for Everyone

I think it's vital to remember always that your home's welcome is not just for visitors. If you or your family and friends usually enter by a different door than guests do, try to make that entrance beautiful, too. Don't underestimate the power of the little touches to make your own family feel at home.

Great First Impressions

☞ Your foyer or entrance hall is a great place for a "love wall." Group plaques and pictures people have given you as gifts into a decorative reminder of how much people care.

☞ For an old-fashioned welcoming touch, try painting your door a bright red, a glossy green, or a shiny black.

☞ Your main entrance can say "welcome" in any season with a May basket, a fall arrangement of Indian corn, or a green wreath at Christmas.

☞ To provide a cozy first impression for the senses, light some candles or use a Christmas potpourri spray throughout the house any time of the year.

☞ Before leaving for a trip, set aside half an hour before you leave to straighten the house so it will greet you with serenity instead of clutter. Your first impression counts too!

Even those little imperfections you hardly notice anymore—the muddy boots by the doorway, the bag of garbage waiting by the door, the broken hinge that reaches out to snag sweaters—can be little irritants that drag your spirit down.

If you live alone, it's very important to create a pleasing first impression. In a sense, your home itself is what welcomes you after a long day. Something as simple as a light turned on by a timer, a radio playing soft music, or dinner in a Crockpot can soften that feeling of coming home to a dark, empty house or apartment. A few minutes of straightening in the morning can take away the stress of coming home to a house full of things to do.

Final impressions can be important, too. I like to have something hanging by the door *on the inside* that says a friendly farewell—perhaps a plaque with a poetic blessing, a mirror to double-check hair or makeup, or a pretty decoration just to say a smiling good-bye.

Coming and Going

The best possible way to greet family and visitors alike is literally with your open arms, or at least with your smiling presence.

Our dear friends Jim and Barbara DeLorenzo like to take this idea of a face-to-face hello even further. They like to sit on their top step with a cool drink, smilingly waiting for their guests to drive up. More eloquently than any words, their eager, welcoming presence says, "We just can't wait to be with you!"

If you have children, you can send them outside to watch for the new arrivals, then ask them to bring the guests inside and take their coats. A spouse or housemate can perform the same welcoming job. Or at the very least, you can put out a sign or banner that ways "Welcome."

You might be amazed at what happens when you take the time to greet your own family with that special "I'm excited to see you" welcome. Why not stroll out to meet your weary spouse at the end of a hard day or walk to the bus stop to greet your children? If everyone comes home together, why not have snacks and drinks in the refrigerator for a little family "happy hour" before the evening starts?

The same applies to everyday good-byes. Instead of a distracted peck or a shouted good-bye, occasionally go for a big hug and a personal escort out the door. Every once in a while, a little wrapped gift or a note slipped into a backpack or a briefcase can start a day off with an extra bit of sunshine.

Coming and going, these special, personal gestures express the spirit of hospitality that makes guests and family alike feel instantly at home. Through your décor, actions, and thoughtfulness you are saying, "I am really glad you came. And I just can't wait until you come back."

Where the Fireplace Glows

THE WARMTH OF SHARED SPACES

*Blest be that spot, where cheerful
guests retire to pause from toil,
and trim their ev'ning pair, and every
stranger finds a ready chair.*

—OLIVER GOLDSMITH

This is the room where the home fires burn the brightest, but the fireplace is optional!

This room is the center of warmth, the gathering place where family members come together gladly and where guests quickly become one of the family. Call it the living room, the den, the family room—the name doesn't really matter. It could be the corner of an efficiency apartment or even, in the right climate, a front porch. Regardless of what you call it, though, every home needs one—a place for people to rest for a bit and share their lives.

I love our great room because it is a living room in the truest sense. We *live* here— we come together in this room to share our lives and share each other's company.

A ROOM OF STORIES

There is plenty of room for memories here. Every object around us tells a story about the events in our lives that have made us who we are.

The faces of people I love smile at me all around this room—sometimes in person, sometimes in memory, and always in the form of photographs that populate every table and hang from the walls as well.

When I take a moment to ponder the many parties and celebrations that have taken place in this room, I just beam with joy: birthdays, gathering of loved ones, an endless parade of Thanksgivings and Christmases (the whole room spangled with lights and fragrant with greenery), Hanukkah celebrations, too, that represented a rediscovery of my Jewish heritage and a reconciliation with family members who had long resented my embracing a different faith.

The everyday moments are equally precious. All around me march a priceless procession of ordinary moments that have defined our ongoing life together. Mothers nursing babies. Children snuggled in their blankies, watching TV or listening to a story. Bob and I close together on the couch, making plans for our next business venture or our next home improvement project. Even the painful moments—the difficult discussions, the frustrating arguments, the times of silence and worry— are part of the memory glow that makes this room home to me.

Not Just for Company

This memory room is a family room. It is also the room where we welcome guests and strangers into our midst and make them part of us. We do not have a special receiving room reserved for "company." When you visit us, you join with us in the warmth of our shared spaces.

I have never liked the idea of maintaining a separate living room where the drapes are kept drawn to protect the upholstery, where children are not allowed to sit on the furniture, where the beautiful objects and "good" furniture gather dust. How can such a situation feel welcoming to either family or guests, when the family is deprived of the beauty of treasured objects and guests are deprived of the warmth of the family hearth?

Why not share your memories, your comfort, your hearth with those who come to visit?

And why not give your best and most beautiful to the people who use the house the most?

Arranged for Welcome

How you arrange your common areas and how you choose the spaces where people will gather depends on you, your budget, and your floor plan. A small dwelling has limited choices. A larger home offers more options and demands more decisions: Do you need a separate music room, sewing room, library, or recreation room?

But regardless of your resources, this basic principle of maintaining an inviting hearth space for family and friends can guide you in creating welcoming rooms that invite people to sit and share their lives.

There may be reasons to separate living spaces according to

Focal Points

- What aspect of your home do you enjoy most: the view, the quiet, the yard? Let that aspect be the focus of your hospitality. Encourage others to share this pleasure.

- If you are lucky enough to have a fireplace, make that the focus of your room. Invest in useful and beautiful tools, attractive boxes for wood, and even utensils for cooking over the fire.

- Rotating your pictures not only keeps a room fresh, but it can also cut down on sun damage. Any picture exposed to sunlight even part of the day should be rotated.

- Set up a card table in the living or family room with a puzzle in progress or games ready to play. This will catch the eye of visitors and family members and invite them to take part in the fun.

- Instead of a traditional lamp table, try stacking a series of sturdy wooden trunks or stenciled packing boxes. An old trunk also serves beautifully for a coffee table and storage.

mood or décor: her dainty floral sun room, for instance, and his rich-looking, leather-bound library. It may also make sense to have separate spaces for different kinds of shared activities so that one person can play the piano while another watches TV, or so that one person can read while another exercises.

But in this day of increasing separation and isolation, isn't it time we rediscovered the art of togetherness, or sharing space and time and memories together? So many family activities can coexist in the same room. Children can play quietly on the rug while Grandma knits or reads a magazine. Dad and Mom can file tax receipts while a guest reads a magazine. Sister can practice the piano while the rest of the family actually listens or sings along.

SHARING THE AREA

In an at-home living area there must be a

comfortable place to sit, perhaps a comfortable place to stretch out, with plenty of cushions or pillows. A carpet or warm rugs provide the kind of "soft floor" that children love and adults appreciate.

It should also be relatively low-maintenance, a place where spills can be tolerated and feet don't always have to stay on the floor. This should also be a beautiful space. Your primary gathering place should be filled with what you and your family love most, whether it's antique flour mills or handmade kaleidoscopes or model airplanes.

In our experience, at least, this process of merging our tastes into a beautiful whole has been a wonderful adventure. We have found that our tastes marry well, and many of our loves coincide: the paintings, the collections of little barns, the antique armoires, the Amish quilts. The key is love, respect, and sometimes a willingness to put up with something that just isn't "you" in favor of a total effect of "we."

What do the people in your family love to do: play music, watch sports, wrestle on the floor? Your living room will be warmer and everyone will feel more at home if you make space for those activities to take place.

Living rooms provide a perfect setting for whole-family activities. For many years when our family was young, Friday nights were family night, when we would pop corn, play games, or just talk and spend time together. Such gatherings can be wonderful, warm uses of a living room.

Being Together or Being Alone

The whole point of a living room is to be at home together. If you set up the space to make room for togetherness, people will be more likely to gather there.

Little touches can make a big difference.

The way the furniture is arranged, for example, can tell a lot about your priorities and your at-home spirit. Does the furniture "turn its back" to a newcomer or block the view of the fire? Are there comfortable groupings for conversation? Does every seat have adequate lighting and a place to put down drinks? Is there room to move without knocking things over or tripping?

And a big question...where is the TV? Many family rooms these days are set up with every chair pointed in the direction of the television. No wonder family time often disintegrates into merely staring at the tube together.

With a little experimentation, you can help play down the TV's role in your shared life. My friend Yoli accomplished this by placing the TV on a high stand in the corner of the room. It's visible from most places, but not an integral part of the furniture grouping. And I know some people who keep theirs on a wheeled cart in the closet, ready to roll out for special occasions.

If space permits, I like to fill a living space with several separate groupings, not only the traditional gathering of sofas and chairs around a coffee table. My mother's wing chair sits over by a little table with a lamp—a nice place to sit and write a letter. A gathering of child-sized chairs and toys invites small people to make themselves at home. Several little tables hold groups of photos and conversation pieces. The breakfast bar with its high stools offers a great area for work or conversation. It's Bob's favorite morning place to read and drink coffee.

I've felt thoroughly welcome and at home in tiny efficiency apartments with furniture crammed wall to wall, or in new, big houses with barely a stick of furniture. I've felt comfortable in homes where children and teenagers were constantly coming in and out the doors, and in quiet, serene homes where one man or woman has lived alone for many years.

What matters, you see, is not the size of the room or the number of people who share the space, but the warmth of the welcome to resident and guest alike.

What matters is the memories, with the stories attached.

What matters is that warm fireside glow—with or without the fire.

Company in the Kitchen

The Joy of Cooking and Sharing Together

My earliest happy memories all seem to be kitchen memories.

In my mind's eye I can see myself, a tiny girl of four or five, perched on a countertop amid mounds of chopped vegetables, countless bottles and jars of spices, dustings of flour. I loved to watch my father as he cooked.

My father was a creative, temperamental Viennese chef. Orphaned at a young age, he had been raised in the kitchens of the palace of Vienna, and the kitchen was his native habitat. In the early 1940s, after he came to America, he worked for Fox Studios in Hollywood. Many of the old-time movie stars—including Clark Gable, Lana Turner, Mario Lanza, and Betty Grable—joined in standing ovations for my father's lavish buffets.

Ever since those days, it seems, my happiest times have involved preparing and serving food in the company of people I love. I treasure my father's stainless-steel ladle, his chef's knife, and his wonderful recipe for olive-oil dressing. And I love an open kitchen where more happens than just meal preparation. To me, the kitchen is the place in the home where many blessings begin: the blessing of nourishment, fellowship, creativity, shared meals, and shared lives.

A Place You Love to Be

Our current kitchen is spacious and convenient, with lots of pantry and cupboard space. I love its look, its glassed-in shelves, its pantry, its handy hangers for pots and pans.

But I don't require a perfect facility to be at home in the kitchen.

I have enjoyed cooking and sharing in many homes and many kitchens, and I have learned that even the smallest of them can be organized, efficient, and inviting.

The key to making the best of any kitchen space is to make efficient use of the space you have. But even more important, I believe, is making it a place you love to be. After all, a large chunk of the average person's lifetime is spent

in food-related activities, and many of those take place in the kitchen. If you are a woman 45 years or older, you've already spent more than 50,000 hours in the kitchen. It is only sensible that you will design your kitchen to be homey and comfortable and beautiful, no matter what its size.

It doesn't take a major remodeling job to make your kitchen a room you enjoy and feel good in. A fresh paint job, new knobs on the cabinet doors, or just a thorough cleaning and rearranging will do wonders. What about a radio on the shelf? Don't forget a kitchen stool to save your back and legs and a step stool to help you reach those high shelves.

It's also essential to make the kitchen a room in which you can work efficiently. Just a little bit of planning can save countless steps and, over the years, many hours of your time.

The simple rule we've always followed in our kitchen is "Things that work together go together." Thus, coffeemaker, coffee, sugar bowl and sweetener, and coffee mugs gather together in one cupboard and counter area. Dish towels live next to the sink, pot holders nestle close to the stove, and wooden spoons and spatulas sprout from their holder next to the stove like a cheerful bouquet, cheerfully inviting me and my friends to "come in and use me."

Everyone Is Family

I love it when my family and guests join me in the kitchen so that we can spend time together while meals are being cooked or special treats are being created. When guests come, they're part of the family, and that means they're with me in the kitchen.

Sometimes they sit and talk while I get dinner underway.

More often, though, I'll put each person to work, and we'll all have fun together.

First, I'll set out a little plate of hors d'oeuvres that I've prepared for all of us to munch on while dinner is being prepared—something simple, like low-fat tortilla chips and salsa, or some fresh vegetables and dip.

Then, perhaps, I'll pull out our big wooden salad bowl and a few cloves of garlic, and I'll set one guest to mashing the garlic into a paste with salt and pepper, then adding olive oil and vinegar and lemon to make my father's special salad dressing. The greens are torn and laid in the bowl on top of the salad dressing. Then come the tomatoes and the onions and the avocado and the green pepper—whatever luscious ingredients are on hand—and the salad is ready to toss.

This especially is the guest's job. I tell him or her, just as my daddy told me, "Toss it until you think it's all mixed. Then toss it some more."

My father always insisted that the tossing was the secret of a good salad. So I was amused and validated to find this Spanish proverb: "Let the salad-maker be a spendthrift for oil, a miser for vinegar, a statesman for salt, and a madman for mixing." Now I guess I'll encourage my company in the kitchen to go just a little mad!

And in the midst of it all, of course, there is talk.

I've had some of my best conversations while I was stirring a pot of soup and someone else was tossing and tossing and tossing that salad.

Good talk just seems to happen naturally in the kitchen, whetted by the repetitive work and the wonderful aromas.

Confidences flow easily in that warm, intimate environment.

Creativity flourishes as people work together.

Teamwork clicks into place as one person puts ice in the glasses and another person pulls the napkins into rings and still another one lights the candles.

No one is lonely. No one feels left out—not even the cook.

And then we can all sit down together with a sense of joy and satisfaction.

Warming the Heart of the Home

- Little lamps in your kitchen are a nice way of adding warm points of light. Try tucking a tiny lamp in a high cabinet with glass doors to showcase some pretty mugs or serving pieces.

- If you have room in the kitchen, why not put in a comfy sitting chair. You'll have more company while you work, and you'll love that chair when your feet give out.

- Pretty cotton dish towels make beautiful napkins, placemats, or even café curtains. Or sew several together and hang them across the top of your window as a cheerful valance.

- On a slow afternoon, put on soft music and browse through your favorite recipe book for ideas and inspiration. Take time to enjoy the mood of your own kitchen.

- Store your frequently used cooking additives, like olive oil and wine vinegar, in decorative decanters and keep your counters free of clutter. The room will look more spacious, more organized, and your time there will be inspired.

CHILDREN AT HOME IN THE KITCHEN

Kitchens are wonderful and irresistible places for children, and ours were in the kitchen from the time they were tiny. I always tried to have some kind of delicious aroma coming from the oven when my children came home from school—just as my mama did for me. And both children have turned out to be wonderful cooks.

Now our grandchildren are my special kitchen friends. Granddaughter Christine and I have been baking cookies together since she was very tiny, and now she is self-assured as she rolls out buttery scones for our tea parties. She also loves to play waitress and take orders: "I'm here to take your drink orders. We have plain water, ice water, and water with lemon...."

Chad is our scrambled-egg chef and is adept at frying bacon and sausage as well. Bevan, who for years has been Chad's assistant, is moving into his own as a cook. And in the past few years the littlest boys have begun to move into the kitchen, too.

At an outdoor family party, for instance, we recruited then three-year-old Bradley Joe as a server. Enchanted by the responsibility, he carefully carried out plates and bowls and utensils. Then he carried out mustard and catsup and mayonnaise and carefully placed them on the table. And then came the soy sauce, the Worcestershire sauce, jars of capers and jalapeños, and cartons of butter, milk, and eggs. He became so excited over his kitchen responsibilities that he was emptying the refrigerator! We were all pleased that at such a young age he was already catching the spirit of the kitchen.

Children need to be in the kitchen not only because it's a center of family warmth, but also because they need to learn kitchen skills. They need to learn to measure and stir and read recipes and plan meals. And they learn so much more at the same time: organization, teamwork, nutrition, even science. (A home-baked loaf of yeast bread is not only a fragrant expression of love, it's also a wonderful lesson in both biology and chemistry: the action of microorganisms, the expansion of gases, the effects of heat on matter, and so much more!)

Yes, having children in the kitchen can be messy. But children are washable, and so is my kitchen. And I consider the extra cleanup time to be a worthwhile investment in a future of happy kitchen hours for myself and this next generation.

I can't wait until the day when I go to visit those children and they invite me into their grown-up kitchens.

Just give me an apron and a chef's hat and hand me the salad bowl.

I'll make like a madman and toss them a salad they won't believe!

Go not abroad
for happiness.
For see it is
a flower that
blooms at
thy door.

—Minot J. Savage

33

Merry Occasions & Movable Feasts

MAKING MEMORIES WITH SPECIAL CELEBRATIONS

Address yourself to entertain them sprightly, and let's be red with mirth.

—WILLIAM SHAKESPEARE

Why have a meal, I've always thought, when you can invest just a little bit more and have a celebration?

I don't mean more money. I mean a little more thought, a little more caring. Sometimes a little more time or energy. Always, a little more sharing and appreciation.

For that's really what a celebration is.

A sharing. An appreciation. A conscious commitment to joy.

Because eating is such a basic part of our existence, the place we eat is the ideal place to celebrate. That should mean the dining room, of course. But I have to admit that we don't eat in our dining room very often.

In our home, mealtime celebrations are a movable feast.

My motto is "Have card table, will travel."

Bob and I have celebrated mealtimes in great rooms, or garden rooms in front of the fire, out by ponds, occasionally in dining rooms, often in breakfast rooms or perched by breakfast bars, and as often as we can out on patios or verandas. We have set up "love feasts" in our bedroom, enjoying special romantic times just for the two of us. We have also set up tables on the lawn to entertain big gatherings of friends and family.

"Eating," writes Alexandria Stoddard, "is the ritual of communion." That's exactly what mealtimes are to Bob and me. They are the times during the day when we sit down together and share our lives—sometimes just with the two of us,

35

sometimes with our family, sometimes with treasured friends—nourishing our spirits and our relationships as well as our bodies.

In a sense, it's the time when we are most at home to ourselves and to anyone who is sharing our lives at the moment.

Everyday Warmth

Our traveling feasts, wherever they take place, are served on pretty dishes (or cheerful paper plates) with cloth napkins. Whenever possible, I like to add a candle or a spray of ivy or a whimsical napkin ring—just a little something to remind us that even everyday eating is a special time of the day.

We turn off the television for mealtime—and it's a good idea to let the answering machine take care of the phone. We avoid bringing our arguments and problems to the table. Mealtime is a time for sharing, but also for peace—a moment in the day when we celebrate togetherness and the gift of nourishment.

If you live alone, setting a pretty table and lighting a candle for an everyday meal can seem like too much trouble, and turning off the television can feel like cutting off your only chance for company.

If you have a busy, active family, just getting everybody to eat at the same time can be difficult.

It's worth the effort, though, for at least one meal a day.

It's worth making the rules, taking the time, preparing the food—even if it's as simple as macaroni and cheese or take-out pizza. It's worth turning off the noise and turning on the soft music and lighting the candles to make the meal feel warmer and more peaceful. It's worth making the effort to talk and share about the day.

Thinking of everyday meals as celebrations is a step toward making yourself and your family more beautifully at home.

If you have plants and flowers around—either real or silk—you will always have something ready for a centerpiece.

If you stock your freezer with frozen casseroles, you'll always have the wherewithal for a spontaneous feast.

If you maintain your home on a regular schedule, it will always look ready for a celebration.

So think ahead just a little bit and set up your life to be ready for a party. When party supplies go on sale at the drugstore, I like to stock up on colored plates and napkins, streamers, little gifts, even party hats and noisemakers. When candles are inexpensive, I buy them in bulk and store them in my freezer (to keep them burning longer and cleaner). I keep a roll of cookie dough in my freezer and some scone mix in the pantry and some wonderful, aromatic coffee or tea on my shelves. And I always keep the teapot clean and shiny, because I never know when the opportunity for a tea party will present itself.

Perhaps it will be a good report card. Or an old friend who calls to say he's in town just for the evening. Or a project that is finished, a crisis that is over. Or I simply realize it's been too long since our last party.

Whatever the reason, I'm ready.

"Big-Deal" Celebrations

Not all of your at-home celebrations will be spur-of-the-moment. Sometimes it is really fun

Planning for Spontaneous Fun

I treasure the memories from times of spontaneous merrymaking, when we decided on the spur of the moment to have a party. But these were almost always more successful with a bit of advance planning.

Sound like a contradiction of terms? It's not. It takes a certain amount of thinking ahead to make spontaneity possible, or at least to widen your possibilities for spontaneous at-home celebrations.

to throw an "event," complete with written invitations, elaborate decorations, and lavish foods. And even a very formal dinner can be gracious and fulfilling, deeply satisfying and filled with the spirit of celebration. Your meticulous planning and loving preparation, your most beautiful tablecloths and place settings and centerpieces—all can be wonderful ways to tell your guests that you care enough to plan for their visit.

A birthday, a holiday, a family reunion—all these can be reasons to pull out the stops and have a party. A "big-deal" celebration can be informal: a barbecue, a pizza party, or even a covered-dish get-together. Or it can be beautifully formal with linen cloth and sparkling crystal.

For me in the last few years, these are the times when I bring out my auntie's beautiful china and crystal, my crisp, white linen tablecloths, my crystal candle holders. These are the times when Jenny helps me arrange beautiful flowers for a centerpiece, when I plan for days in advance, when I write place cards and plan little gifts for each guest. We don't do this very often in our home—we really live quite informally—but we treasure these times of special celebration in our lives.

Don't let the prospect of such a celebration daunt you.

The only requirements are beauty and warmth and a little bit of extra effort.

At-Home Celebrations

🌿 Make celebration a tradition in your family. Celebrate everything: good days, bad days that are finally over, birthdays, nonbirthdays, milestones, accomplishments, anything.

🌿 For a festive touch at the table, "gift-wrap" the place settings with wide ribbon or strips of gauze. Stack plate, salad plate, bowl, and glass on top of two crossed ribbons. Gently bring ribbons up around the place setting and tie in a big, floppy bow.

🌿 Celebrate your family's cultural heritage—Italian, Scottish, Mexican, Chinese, or American heartland—with a special kind of dinner party. Serve native foods, play music of that heritage, even learn a folk dance or a custom to share with others.

🌿 Just once during the summer, turn dinner into a celebratory time by serving sundaes or banana splits as your main meal. This rare indulgence will spark lots of smiles and laughter.

🌿 Share the touch of home with others. Several times a year create a "love basket" filled with food for a needy family. Or try spending part of your holidays helping a local mission or shelter.

Intimate Spaces

THE REST AND ROMANCE OF THE BEDROOM

Take thou of me, sweet pillows, sweetest bed...A rosy garland and a weary head.

—SIR PHILIP SIDNEY

You can see it in your dreams—this beautiful, restful, romantic place that is all your own.

This is the blissful bower where you take your weary body for a rejuvenating catnap, a peaceful night of slumber, or a restful moment with a favorite book. It's a pampering retreat where you let yourself be refreshed and renewed and readied to start again.

Your bedroom is the place where you can go and shut the door and be most deeply you. Shouldn't they be the most beautiful, the most welcoming, the most inviting rooms in your house?

Unfortunately, though, they are often just the opposite.

As a society, we are impatient with the idea of rest. We are uncomfortable with closeness and intimacy. For all our talk about "taking care of ourselves," we tend to focus on our outer lives and neglect our inner ones.

All too often, these rooms are the afterthoughts of the house. They are the last to be decorated, the first to fill up with clutter.

The master bedroom becomes the place where the clothes baskets and the mail pile up. Dressers are piled high, the television blares, and toys clutter the floor. Sometimes there is a crib, a playpen, an ironing board, or a baby swing. The bathroom, too, especially a private bathroom, becomes a place where hand-washables dangle or magazines pile up in a corner.

Most of us spend an average of ten hours a day in our bedrooms and baths—dressing, undressing, exercising, reading, reflecting, sewing, writing, puttering, talking on the phone or watching television, playing with children, sleeping, eating, putting on makeup, and so on. At this rate we could and will spend half our lives in our bedrooms—and we spend one-third of our lives actually in bed! If at all possible, therefore, these rooms

whatever quiets and relaxes you. Consider the feel of the sheets—cool cotton or cozy flannel. Scent the air with potpourri or candles or even incense. Toss a woolly afghan over the end of the bed or on a chair to wrap around you for a nap. A good lamp by the bedside invites you to read in bed. A radio or tape recorder nearby lifts your spirits with beautiful music or keeps you company with quiet talk.

In past years I have slept in many different rooms—in hotels and homes and wonderful bed-and-breakfast places. But I never rest quite as well as when I am in my very own restful retreat center.

I am never quite so at-home as when I am in my very own beautiful bed.

A Setting for Romance

But it's not just my bedroom, of course.

I share this room with my Bob, the love of my life, my partner in work and play and romance. And we both value our bedroom as the site of our most intimate sharing.

When we come in here, the door closes behind us.

No matter who is in the rest of the house, here it's just the two of us, and here is where we nurture the inner life of our marriage.

We spend hours talking and dreaming—building our closeness by sharing our hearts. We make love here. We read to each other from the books by our bedside. Sometimes we bring in a tray and enjoy a cup of tea or a cozy breakfast in bed, or we set up the card table and enjoy a leisurely romantic dinner.

should be your most beautiful private sanctuary. They should be the first rooms you decorate, making them all you wish them to be. They should be serene and beautiful—rooms that invite you to peaceful, intimate sharing.

A Place to Retreat

It helps to think of your bedroom as your own personal retreat center—a place where quiet beauty wraps itself around you and slumber beckons, a place where you can kick off your shoes and shed the stress of the day.

Ask yourself what kind of atmosphere you want to create. A garden of soft pastels and greens? Bright colors that give you energy? Perhaps an earthy collage of rusts, golds, and browns, or a seascape of clear blue and sunny pastels? Whatever the colors and the decorations, make this the happiest and most restful room in your world.

Let your five senses lead you, and include

For this truly is a romantic room—a place not only of love, but of sensual delight, of delicious textures and beautiful sights and sensuous aromas and wonderful tastes. We work to keep it that way with soft lighting, smooth sheets, and fresh flowers.

We try to keep our conversations uplifting, not putting each other down. We make time for one another and make it a priority to be sensitive to each other. Bob and I have had many happy times in our room, and some difficult, heart-hurting times as well. But the memories bring smiles when we've shared the true spirit of refuge and romance in our private space.

DREAMS COMING TRUE

Do your private rooms welcome you? Have you expended the same effort for the places where you retreat as you have for

Susan Ries

the places where you welcome guests? My bedroom is one of the places I go to find stillness. Here I can shut the door and find space to be quiet, to read and think and dream. Sometimes I will write in my journal, letting my thoughts grow clearer as they distill on the page. Often I will meditate or pray, letting my spirit be renewed. Sometimes I simply lie still and breathe deeply, enjoying the solitude.

We all need a place for private, intimate aloneness—a place where we can be at home in the stillness and come to know ourselves for who we really are. If our private rooms are lovely and romantic and inviting, our inner lives will be nourished, and our outer lives cannot help but be better.

Are you happy and at home in your most intimate space and your most intimate relationships?

If that is true, you will have a home base for beauty and serenity, a spiritual center for at-homeness.

Your private chambers will be the place where your at-home dreams come true.

Fit for a Princess

Come in the evening, or come in the morning,
Come when you're looked for, or come without warning,
Kisses and welcome you'll find here before you,
And the oftener you come here the more I'll adore you.

—THOMAS O. DAVIS (from an Irish proverb)

Once upon a time, there was a beautiful young girl named Jenny who dreamed of being a princess. She loved to listen to those wonderful stories about princesses of old— and the room where she slept and dreamed and made herself at home became known as the Princess Room.

Eventually, Princess Jenny—our daughter—grew up and went off to college. She packed up her bags and left the Princess Room behind—but it wasn't empty long.

That pretty, comfortable room soon became the place where guests stayed when they came to spend the night. They would smile and get a little excited when they were told, "Oh, you get to sleep in the Princess Room."

THE ROYAL TREATMENT

We want our guests to feel like royalty. Our hope is for them to feel pampered, appreciated, and loved.

And we want this kind of royal hospitality to be built into the fabric of our everyday lives, so that on the spur of any moment we can say, "Please come and spend time with us."

To us, hospitality is so much more than entertaining, so much more than menus and decorating and putting on a show. Instead, it's a matter of organizing our lives so there's always room for one more— always an extra place at the table or an extra pillow and blanket, always a welcome for those who need a listening ear or a place to stay the night.

You certainly don't need a special room just for guests. Hospitality can

thrive in the simplest of settings and the humblest of circumstances. It's a matter of opening your life to others, giving them the best you have to offer, but never allowing elaborate preparations to substitute for an open-armed welcome.

HOSPITABLE ESSENTIALS

The key to successful hospitality is being sensitive to the needs of your guests, and you can do that in any setting, especially with a little bit of advance planning. Both the way you set up your guest quarters and the way you treat your guests when they arrive can make visiting your home a royal experience.

What are the essentials of overnight hospitality?

The most important thing, of course, is a comfortable place to sleep. The ideal is a comfortable bed with a quality mattress and foundation. A quality sofa bed or futon provides a good alternative, especially if you supplement these thinner mattresses with a foam mattress or an "egg crate" mattress pad. Be sure you personally try out your guest bed, sofa bed, futon, or cot. If you can't get a good night's sleep there, your guests won't either.

Always provide fresh linens for an overnight guest. Sheets of fine-grained cotton or even silk in the summer or fuzzy flannel in the winter raise the comfort level a notch. So can embroidered pillowcases and large, plush towels. An extra blanket, a comforter, or a fan can be a godsend if the temperature changes suddenly in the night.

After a comfortable sleeping place, a guest needs privacy—room to dress and think and retreat. If you have a separate guest room, this is easy. If not, a little ingenuity can provide your guests with space. It's a good idea, for example, to set up your guest bed in a room that is not needed on an everyday basis. Perhaps an office or a den could serve as temporary guest quarters, abandoning its usual purpose for the space of a visit. If guests must sleep in a more public area (such as the sofa), take care to keep the family elsewhere some of the time, giving guests a little while to relax in peace.

It's always helpful if you clear away some of your own things to make space for your guest. If possible, empty out a part of a closet and a drawer or two. At the very least, set aside a corner for luggage and provide some hooks for hanging coats and dresses. In the bathroom, a rack or hook for special towels and some counter space for toiletries will be appreciated.

GOLDEN RULE HOSPITALITY

Once these basics are provided, some imaginative extra touches can make a big difference. These are the little extras that say "I care."

An adequate, well-placed reading light plus an assortment of books and current magazines help guests prepare for sleep. A comfortable chair provides a place to relax or to put on shoes. A good clock radio provides both music and a sense of independence, while a bowl of fruit or a pitcher of water takes care of midnight munchies.

And beautiful objects—fresh flowers, lovely pictures, scented candles, interesting mementos—help create a welcoming and personal atmosphere.

book or magazine I love on the bedside table or a simple gift in a beautifully wrapped package.

And I love to bring my guests a morning tray. This has become almost a trademark of the "Barnes' bed and breakfast." A fragrant cup of coffee or tea or a steaming mug of cocoa served with toast and jelly accompanied by a little candle is a simple way to make anyone feel special—a wonderful affirmation of the joy of sharing your lives through hospitality.

There are so many hospitable extras that can make your guests' stay a royal experience. You just need a little empathy, a little imagination, a little creativity, plus a willingness to make sharing your life and your home a priority.

Not Just for Company

I really believe that treating people like royalty should be an everyday practice extended to those who share our lives as well as those who come to visit.

A few summers ago, while we were on vacation, my Bob injured his knee playing tennis. Several days after we arrived home, the pain became so intense that Bob decided to spend the morning in bed. Here, at last, was an opportunity for me to share hospitality and prepare breakfast in bed for my Bob—something I often do for overnight guests. The tray was splendid with fresh, hot coffee in a pretty china cup and saucer, steaming bran muffins, fruit and

But royal treatment is not just a matter of how you prepare for guests. It is also a matter of what you do for your guests while they are with you. If I have time, for instance, I like to sneak into the guest room after dinner and turn down the sheets. (I have even been known to leave a mint.) I refresh the supply of towels in the bath and empty the wastebasket. I leave a copy of a

coconut, granola, fresh-squeezed orange juice, a vase of freshly picked flowers, and a candle.

As I fluffed up the pillows and placed the tray on his lap, Bob's smile said it all. "How beautiful!" he exclaimed. "And just for me?" Weeks later, he still spoke of his breakfast in bed.

I realized it was the first time in more than 35 years I had ever awakened my Bob, whom I love so deeply, with a beautiful breakfast tray. Since that occasion I've decided to try giving Bob the royal treatment more often, even when he's perfectly healthy.

It really doesn't take much to give anybody the princess treatment, and the payoffs are immense in terms of warm hospitality, enriched friendships, and widened horizons.

It's just one more step toward living happily and comfortably ever after.

Extra! Extra! The Special Touch for Guests

🌿 Breakfast in bed—even as simple as cinnamon toast and a perfect cup of tea or coffee—will make a guest feel like royalty. Add a sprig of flowers and note of welcome to brighten their morning and their stay.

🌿 A big hit in our guest bathroom is a big, fluffy terry robe hanging on the back of the bathroom door. If you love that touch in fancy hotels, why not invest in one for your home?

🌿 Save the complimentary bottles of shampoo and lotion, the little sewing kits, and shoeshine cloths you receive in hotels. Add a toothbrush and toothpaste and tuck these items into a little basket for your guest bathroom.

🌿 An extra touch includes having the basics covered. Do you have plenty of toilet paper, towels, washcloths, soap?

🌿 If your guest is an old friend, pull out a picture of the two of you together, tuck it into an antique frame, and place it on the bedside table.

Always a Place to Play

A House that Welcomes Children

God looks down well pleased to mark
In earth's dusk each rosy spark,
Lights of home and lights of love,
And the child the heart thereof.

—KATHERINE TYNAN

I don't believe in child-proofing my home. To me, that sounds as if children and home are natural enemies—as if they need to be protected from one another. And I just don't believe that's true. At least, that has never been true for me—and at one time in my life our house was home for five children under six years of age!

Even today, our nest is far from empty as far as children are concerned. Our five grandchildren and their friends are frequent visitors. Other children come with their parents for one reason or another. And I've never felt that I had to make my house "proof" against any of these small guests. Instead, I want them to feel a part of everything we're doing. They add an incredible richness and vitality to our lives and to our home by helping to make it a friendly and welcoming place to be.

And we take precautions to be sure little ones are safe and sound. It's not the concept of home safety that I object to, but the sound of the term *childproofing*. I prefer child-friendly!

I have discovered that a child-friendly house is friendlier to the child within me.

When I surround myself with childlike things—with vintage toys and lovely dolls and whimsical books—I find that my spirit stays fresher, more playful, more spontaneous and loving.

My whole life is not only richer but more lighthearted, more comforted. I feel safer and more protected when I infuse my home with a childlike spirit.

So a child-friendly house is a place where you can learn, a place where you can make mistakes and be forgiven.

It's a place where you can explore, where you can share, where you can always find something that is just your size in a world that often feels too big.

It's a place to pretend, a place where imagination and creativity flourish.

It's a place to work.

But always, always, there's a place to play.

That's the kind of house that

welcomes children of all ages—the kind of house that always feels delightfully at-home.

Equipping a Home to Be Child-Friendly

What does it take to make a home child-friendly?

At the most basic level, it begins with remembering what it's like to be a child and what children like. Children love to pretend and imagine and create. They love being able to have adventures within safe limits. They respond to beauty with enthusiasm and learn with gusto, especially if the learning is accompanied with praise and a sense of accomplishment.

The most basic way to establish a child-friendly atmosphere in any home is to keep a few (or many) classic, time-proven toys in a place where every child can find them.

I keep an emergency box on hand with quiet activities to amuse a child who might happen to accompany her mother on a visit. I maintain a supply of crayons, coloring books, simple games, and books for all ages. I also like to keep a supply of small gifts—barrettes, stickers, little flashlights—to send home. And I always have juice in the refrigerator and peanut butter in the pantry—dependable, child-friendly snacks.

Child-Sized Spaces

Children love spaces and furniture that are just their size. Automatically they gravitate to cozy little caves and scaled-down nooks in which they can curl up and play. If there are secret spaces or hidey-holes, all the better.

The child in me immediately said, "Aha" when I saw the tidy little loft above our kitchen and entryway in our home in Riverside. I knew that wonderful little space would be a perfect child headquarters for our house. So with imagination and some sheets that were on sale, my daughter and I created a dream playhouse. We simply added hand-me-down furniture and some play-day basics: a child-sized table and chairs, a wicker cradle full of baby dolls, shelves full of games and stuffed animals, and a giant-sized Winnie the Pooh to keep an eye on things.

A couple of child-sized rocking chairs in a cozy corner next to a basket of books work as wonderfully as a separate playroom. So will a beanbag chair on a rug by the fire with a checker-board hanging on the wall. And there's always the time-tested option of a couple of blankets draped over a card table to create a cozy and welcoming nest. Very few children can resist that kind of a small, dark cave. On a really hectic day, you may find yourself crawling in as well.

Wide, Open Spaces

The outdoors is a child's native habitat, and most children are out the door the minute the opportunity presents itself. Even a tiny yard can provide a child with a place to explore and have fun. All a child really needs is raw materials for their imagination.

A mattress box rescued from the recycling bin will provide any child with hours of fun.

A few sturdy plastic yard toys from a garage sale will say to a child, "I care about you, too."

Or why not outfit small visitors with a shovel and a place they can dig in the garden?

Better yet, put on your gardening togs and invite a child to come work with you. As you do, you will be establishing another vital element of a child-friendly home: You will be establishing a space where the generations live and work and learn together and where one generation can teach another what it means to establish strong, warm, welcoming households.

Homes, you see, are learning labs for "at-homeness." They are where children learn both by teaching and example what it means to take care of themselves and other people. A welcoming home is an ideal teaching space where a child can learn not only social graces, but also the dynamics of working and living with others.

Yours, Mine, and Ours

In our home, we have always assigned home responsibilities according to the "yours, mine, and ours" principle.

Each person in a household, for instance, needs some personal, private "yours" space. Depending on the household, this may be a bedroom and bath, part of a room, or just a bed and a footlocker, but it is yours to decorate and organize as you see

fit. If you want to hang horse posters or athletic pennants on your bedroom walls or paint your personal bathroom yellow and black, that's your decision. But you also have the responsibility to keep it clean and organized. When you are little, I will help you and teach you how to do this: how to make the bed, to put away belongings, to establish a place for everything. But as you grow, the goal will be for you to take responsibility for doing these things yourself.

A child-friendly house should also meet the needs of the adults. There are magazines on the coffee table, lamps on the side table, and plants in the corner. In my case, there are bone-china teacups on open shelves and even on small carts within arm's reach of small explorers.

I wanted all children to experience the joy of living among beautiful things and to learn to care for those things. In my experience, even very young children can learn this lesson happily and proudly—especially when they are introduced to treasures under supervision, allowed to touch and admire, then provided with age-appropriate toys and a place where they can play.

I always stress that I know accidents can happen and that if one of these treasures should break, it's all right, because children are far more precious than any piece of china or glass.

To me, the real treasures of any home are the people of all size who are growing, creating, playing, sharing, and learning there. These are the treasures that truly make a house a home.

The Fun of Alfresco

BRINGING THE OUTDOORS IN AND THE INDOORS OUT

*Light is sweet, and it pleases
the eyes to see the sun.*

—ECCLESIASTES 1:9

I am a better person, a happier person, when I am in close daily contact with the outdoors.

Sunshine, flowers, a fresh breeze, something green—all these outdoor blessings help keep my feet on the ground and my spirits high. And I always feel more at home in my house when I am able to bring a touch of the outdoors into our home—or, even better, to make the outdoors a part of our home.

I've felt that way ever since I was a little girl, and I'll bet you have, too. Remember the days when morning shot you out of the house like a cannon, eager to spend as many hours as possible in the sunshine? Remember running through sprinklers and digging in the dirt and begging your mother for a picnic?

You felt that way because you were made that way. I truly believe we humans were designed to crave the outdoors

and to yearn for outdoor living. For most of us, food tastes better, friendship feels warmer, days seem a little brighter, when we are living alfresco.

Alfresco—that's the Italian word for "outdoors." But the literal meaning of the word is even more inviting. *Alfresco* actually means "in the cool" or "in the freshness." And doesn't that sound like a delicious, delightful place to be?

LIVING ALFRESCO

Our cool veranda in Riverside, shaded by movable awnings and the sparkling poplar trees that were a birthday present from Bob to me, was a lush place to read on a hot afternoon, an idyllic spot to enjoy a pasta dinner with friends. And Bob's garden, with its neat raised containers, its fruit trees, its rose arbors, was a delight for evening strolls with the grandchildren. So were the cinder paths that circle our property under the trees. Ever since we began our life together, we have been finding ways to bring the outdoors into our home and to let our indoor life out into the outdoor freshness.

57

When we bought our first little tract home and began gardening, we were really able to explore ways to blend the outdoors with our daily living. Bob comes from a farming family, but we still were learning together what it takes to build an outdoor paradise in a hot, dry climate. Right away, however, we created a patio with an overhang so we could enjoy meals outdoors.

In that first little home, we also decided to get creative in terms of bringing the outdoors in. We took a little front bedroom off our entry hall and put in bamboo straw matting, a water fountain, lots of ferns, and a little couch. We made a little lanai (a Hawaiian sitting room) out of that bedroom. I kept my sewing machine there, and we also put in a little table so we could enjoy indoor picnics.

We know that life isn't a picnic.

But we never ever want to live our lives without the possibility of a picnic—indoors or out. We have never felt truly at home unless the outdoors was part of our lives.

Bringing the Outdoors In

So how do you make yourself and others at home, alfresco?

You can start with bringing the outdoors in.

Open a window and let the fresh breeze play. Or at the very least, open the curtains and invite the sunshine indoors.

Windows allow the outdoors to smile into your living space. Whenever possible, give them room to shine instead of weighing them down with heavy drapes or elaborate window treatments.

Houseplants are also a wonderful way to bring the outdoors in. They are naturals for cleaning the air and refreshing the spirit, and there's a houseplant suitable for every shade of green thumb.

You don't even need living plants, though, to give that indoor-outdoor feeling to your home. Floral fabrics and botanical prints, for instance, can make the darkest interiors bloom. I love fabrics printed with ivy, roses, violets, and mischievous little pansies (my favorites).

Gifts from the Garden

One of my very favorite ways of bringing the outdoors in is to gather in the fruits of our garden.

What a joy to carry in an apron-full of fresh greens, tomatoes, lemons, or avocados, to wash them and slice them and then taste their sunny freshness.

What a thrill to bring in a single rose or a basket of daisies, trim their stems, and give them a new home in a crystal vase.

And what a privilege to have participated in the growth of these beautiful outdoor things.

I am fortunate to be married to an accomplished and dedicated gardener, and the fruit of his planning and labor enriches the life of our whole family. But you don't have to be a gardener on a large scale to have the pleasure of bringing in food from the outdoors. Even a foot-square plot by the porch planted in tulips or peppers can yield a surprising harvest. A single tomato plant in a tub on the patio can keep you in fresh vegetables all summer. A pot of herbs on the windowsill can flavor your food and your outlook.

FURNISHING YOUR OUTDOOR LIFE

If you are lucky enough to have a large porch, patio, or deck, your options for inside-out living are many. We have never regretted the outdoor areas we have constructed; in fact, we seem to spend more and more time in these spaces every year. But you don't have to spend a fortune on decking and lawn furniture to enjoy an alfresco life.

You can sit on the front step to watch the world go by.

You can fire up a hibachi on the balcony or just lean over the railing to enjoy the sunrise.

If you find that you enjoy this kind of indoor-outdoor living, you might want to invest in furniture that makes it all a little easier. Wicker is traditional and delightful for front porches and other outdoor spaces that are protected from the rain.

A porch swing or lawn swing is guaranteed to bring out the child in anyone, and an hour or so of quiet rocking at twilight, while fireflies flicker and children play nearby can easily transport you to earlier, less-stressful times.

And when the weather simply won't permit an outdoor sojourn, the outdoor celebration can move indoors once more.

A cool salad of homegrown tomatoes and basil while the sun beats down outside.

A sunny bouquet on a rainy autumn afternoon.

A dreamy hour in a comfortable chair with a catalog full of roses.

Indoors or out, it's the freshest, most lovely way to make a house a home.

59

The Business of Living

CREATING A HOSPITABLE WORK SPACE

*The homeliest tasks get beautiful
if loving hands do them.*

—LOUISA MAY ALCOTT

I truly love the idea of my house being a respite, a cozy bed-and-breakfast experience for people who visit us.

But we're not on vacation when we live here!

This is not a summer home where our primary activity is lounging on the patio or popping burgers on the grill. Our home is a place where the real work of living goes on—and I believe that's true for every at-home home. Clothes are cleaned, folded, and mended. Meals are prepared. Packages are wrapped. Toilets are scrubbed. Flowers are arranged.

Increasingly, too, our home is where the work of making a living goes on. Like growing numbers of people, Bob and I maintain a home-based business. Here is where we make calls, send faxes, prepare seminars, and write books.

Your circumstances are probably different, but chances are that

your house, too, is a working house.

Your home is a hospital, where splinters are removed and "boo-boos" are bandaged.

It's a mailing and wrapping center, where packages are prepared and sent.

It's an office, where bills are paid and letters are written.

It's a child-development center, where the next generation is nurtured and trained.

All this means that in a truly welcoming and inviting home, some thought needs to be given to where and how that work will be done. You need a place and a plan for making, fixing, cleaning, and creating things—and for feeling joyfully at home in the process.

A separate room for work is a wonderful luxury, but a lap desk and a set of baskets or a hidden bookshelf or a big box under the bed will do the trick.

The kitchen, of course, is the dedicated workroom for the business of making food, conversation, and camaraderie. And in our kitchen, we have a kind of "command center" with a phone, a message board, an address book, and pictures of the grandchildren.

60

But we have several other areas in our home that beckon us to do what needs to be done with a joyous and willing spirit.

WORKING IN BEAUTY

Beauty is as necessary in the places where you do your work as it is in the places where you talk and sleep and play.

I truly believe that work, even the sometimes tedious work of keeping a home, was meant to be a joy, not a burden. It is the place where our creativity shines, where we garner the fun of achievement. So many of us now enjoy a morning commute to work that is the length our hallway. When going to the "office" involves remaining at home, it is important to make the area comfortable and welcoming...as much so as our places for rest and fellowship.

I don't mean we have to put little ruffled skirts on our fax machines or paint all our mop buckets to match the wallpaper. But it's just as easy to buy (or make) a cheerfully printed ironing-

board cover as a plain gray one. It's not all that time-consuming to cover cardboard storage boxes with contact paper or fabric. Even a battered old desk looks better with some family photos and a little vase of flowers on it.

In my actual office, I find that a beautiful work space is absolutely essential to maintaining a willing spirit. I cover the walls with memorabilia, pepper the shelves with family photos as well as books, and gather plants around me. I use colorful file folders both to cheer me and keep me organized.

Although I have done a lot of work on card tables and folding desks, I work much more comfortably and meaningfully with a "real" desk. A supportive, "ergonomic" chair is absolutely necessary to making me feel welcome in my own work space. So is adequate lighting.

This principle of taking work seriously but allowing it to be beautiful carries over into the work for running a household, too. I have always felt that having "real" tools for housework dignifies these very necessary and worthy tasks, as well as reducing the time it takes to do them. I use a squeegee, an ostrich-feather duster, and a professional-size mop and bucket.

And yet I'm not "all business" when I'm doing housework. I like to have lovely music on the stereo while I'm doing my work, and I like to use my housework time as a time to enjoy the comfort and beauty that surrounds me in my home. Then, when I'm through, I can tuck my tools away in their proper place in the utility room and enjoy the increased comfort and beauty that comes from a carefully tending my nest.

A Welcoming Spot to Work

What kind of work goes on in your home? With just a little thought and planning, you can create a space that helps you do it with joy and enthusiasm.

I don't just mean maintenance chores or work-at-home jobs, either. I also am talking about labors of love: hobbies, crafts, avocations, such as calligraphy, knitting, writing.

No matter what your work, it seems, you need two things.

First, you need a comfortable place to do the work. For many kinds of pursuits, a place to work will mean a usable work surface: a desk, a shop table, or a drafting board. But it may simply be a comfortable chair next to a bright lamp. If possible, it should be permanent and "real"— a desk rather than a folding table, an office chair rather than one borrowed from the kitchen table, a drafting table or board instead of the breakfast bar, a small sewing-machine cabinet rather than the kitchen table. But I certainly wouldn't advise waiting for professional equipment before starting on a work you love. You can start where you are and go from there.

The amount you invest in a work space will depend on how much money you have to spend, how much space you can set aside, how much room the work demands, and how much time you plan to spend working there.

A Time and a Place

Even though you need a certain amount of inviting work space in your house, you don't want your entire home to be a work space. How can your home be a respite if everywhere you look you see nothing but tasks that need doing?

This can be a problem for people who earn their living from their homes. If not controlled, paperwork can migrate onto bedside tables, living room chairs, and kitchen counters. But this can also happen to hobby projects, to household equipment, and to unopened mail.

In order to keep a healthy balance between work and relaxation, there needs to be a way of dividing the two, of saying to yourself and the world, "I'm off-duty now."

If you have separate work space, it may be as simple as shutting the door or putting up a screen.

If you are using the kitchen table, it may simply be a matter of putting the paintbrushes away and placing the canvases on a high shelf to dry.

If you live in a tiny efficiency apartment, it might mean turning off the computer, shutting off the desk light, filing the papers away, and going across the room to light a candle.

In any home, it's a matter of putting away the mop and the broom, putting the spray bottles back under the counter, and taking a deep, satisfied breath.

Work time is over. You've done it beautifully and joyfully, in a work space that welcomed you to the business of living.

Now, for the house and for yourself, it's time for a well-deserved rest.

An Evolving Dream

Every change of scene becomes a delight.
—Seneca

My at-home dreams have evolved. My home has evolved along with them. And I have thoroughly enjoyed the process.

A home is never really finished as long as living people fill it. Don't be afraid to change your home as your needs and priorities change. In fact, I think it's a good idea to keep thinking and planning ahead for change. I don't mean living in the chaos of constant construction or waiting a year to put up pictures in a new apartment. In fact, I think it's important to get a new space put together as quickly as possible, to put your personal touch on it and make it home.

But don't be compelled to have it all perfect or "finished." Leave room for something new. Experiment. Try out new ideas. You can always change them back! Get rid of items that don't work, and always be on the search for ideas that will make your living space more beautiful and welcoming.

But above all, think in terms of your evolving dreams. Think of a welcoming, relaxing haven that offers peace and beauty to everyone who comes inside, guest and visitor alike. Think of making yourself at home and then reaching out to make other people at home, too.

And then, by all means...dream on.